T0165607

EXPERIENCING *the* BLESSINGS *and* GOOD FRUIT *of* CANCER

Countless Blessings, Lessons Learned,
Improved Self Esteem,
Blessing Others, Spiritual Growth

JUDY J. STAMEY

WestBow
PRESS
A DIVISION OF THOMAS NELSON

WestBow Press books may be ordered through booksellers or by contacting:

WestBow Press
A Division of Thomas Nelson
1663 Liberty Drive
Bloomington, IN 47403
www.westbowpress.com
1 (866) 928-1240

ISBN: 978-1-4908-1548-0 (sc)
ISBN: 978-1-4908-1547-3 (e)

Library of Congress Control Number: 2013921021

Printed in the United States of America.

WestBow Press rev. date: 11/20/2013

DEDICATION

"To God be the Glory"

Wade,

> The love of my life with whom I have been blessed to share fifty three years of marriage filled with love, friendship, and happiness. Thank you for always believing in me and encouraging me to do my best in every ministry. Your walk with God has helped me to understand more fully that "I can do all things through Him who strengthens me." Phil 4:13

Lisa,

> Our first born whom God allowed us to love and nurture until her untimely death caused by a rare form of scalp cancer was an inspiration. Lisa's journey with cancer continues to inspire and bless me in every circumstance. She taught me that in the storms of life, we must learn to dance in the rain, not asking God "why me" but "why not me".

Kim and Angel

> Daughters are blessings beyond measure and I am so grateful to be the mother of two beautiful and Godly women. Your love, care, and concern are precious gifts which continue to motivate me to strive harder to get well. I will treasure all the sacrifices you have made to be with me every step of the way.

Cameron, Samantha and Julian

The blessings of grandchildren are immeasurable gifts from God. The unconditional love, smiles and prayers of their youth lifted my spirits on the worst of days. I'll never forget one of the prayers at mealtime, "God, thank you for my Granna, please don't let her die…"

Grandchildren are like a crown to older people.
And children are proud of their parents. Proverbs 17:6 (NIRV)

ACKNOWLEDGMENTS

My heart is filled with gratitude to every person who invested in my life with encouragement, inspiration, and support throughout this difficult journey. Your expressions of love were amazing! Every card, email, gift, meal, and visit lifted my spirit and allowed me to see God in the flesh.

I want to thank the following individuals for encouraging me to share with others how cancer was overshadowed with countless blessings and experiences and for taking the time to read and edit the manuscript before publication. Your suggestions made a significant contribution, and I am indebted to each of you.

BETH BOCK, a retired school teacher, who was an inspiration to our high school classmates, and continues to inspire them, as well as me to do our best. Although a thousand miles separate us, it is amazing that our friendship seems to grow deeper each day.

DONNA BOWMAN, a minister, who inspired me as a student, who excelled in her studies as a doctoral student at Southwestern Baptist Seminary. As one of her professors, I continually give thanks that she blesses me as a colleague, friend and mentor. Donna's generosity of time and ministry actions have blessed me more than words can say.

JOHNNY SUE FARIES, a prayer warrior and dear friend that has only been in my life for a couple of years, but has become a spiritual influence that challenges me to stay focused on the mission of service that God called me to many years ago. Her radiant smile reflects the love of God in a mighty way and every time we're together, it is as if God just made a visit.

PAM WILSON, a special friend and member of my Sunday Morning Bible study class who quietly ministered to me from the time of surgery, chemo treatments, and radiation. Her actions were perfectly planned and administered. It was as if God had whispered in her ear what I needed and when I needed it. Pam has been an example of Jesus illustration, "I was sick and you visited me."

SANDI BLACK, a member of my Sunday Morning Bible study class whose positive influence has been a blessing in many ways. Her smile, words of encouragement and experience with cancer were gifts she shared that helped me to better understand the journey I was on and gave me courage to press on.

NAN DEAN, the first lady at Travis Avenue Baptist Church, who provides such a great example for women. I look up to her, even though she is so much younger. Nan never calls attention to herself, but vigorously serves Christ with a joy that overflows and touches all that come in contact with her. She is a mentor for many that she will never know.

WES BLACK AND JODY PANCOAST, who provided resources that have made the book a reality. Their expertise is reflected throughout the content, and I am grateful for their willingness to work with me.

CONTENTS

Preface xi

CHAPTER 1: Countless Blessings During Cancer 1
Introduction
The Blessing of a Mammogram
The Blessing of Family
The Blessing of Having a Church Family
The Blessing Of Friends And Neighbors
Friendship Is Love With Wings

CHAPTER 2: Lessons Learned from Cancer 19
Introduction
Lesson One: Self Centered Thoughts Dispelled
Lesson Two: Why Me? Why Not Me?
Lesson Three: Following Instructions
Lesson Four: No Hair? Bald?
Lesson Five: Intimacy with My Husband

CHAPTER 3: Self Esteem Issues During Cancer 27
Introduction
Self Esteem and Our Inner Critic
Self Esteem and Being Kind to Yourself
Self Esteem and Looks

CHAPTER 4: How Cancer Can Bless Others 33
Introduction
Popcorn Ministry
Vocational Ministry
Relay for Life Ministry

CHAPTER 5: Spiritual Growth Through Cancer.................. 41
    Introduction
    Overcoming Fear
    Personal Bible Study and Prayer
    Corporate Worship and Small Group Involvement
    Ministering to Others
    Increased Faith and Trust In God
    Bold Witness for Christ

CONCLUSION 51

PREFACE

EXPERIENCING THE BLESSINGS AND GOOD FRUIT OF CANCER

Countless Blessings...Lessons Learned...Improved Self Esteem, Blessing Others...Spiritual Growth

When you hear the dreaded words **"You have cancer"**, it is not unusual to think about the consequences of this dreaded disease. How long will I live? Does this mean surgery? What treatments can be used to eradicate the cancer? How successful are these treatments?

It takes time for a person to process the diagnosis. In addition to the information the doctor has given you, many will explore websites to review the experiences of others who have had a similar cancer, hoping that the information will be helpful in the days and months ahead. However, it's important to remember that every person's experience is unique and much of what you read will not be your experience.

My research led me to information overload, which increased my anxiety about what I may or may not experience. Therefore, I made a decision to accept my journey with breast cancer in its uniqueness and document each step of the way as a means of providing information for our daughters. However, after several entries, I began to realize that what I had perceived as the most difficult time in my life was being overshadowed by an outpouring of God's love. I had claimed his promise of being my refuge and strength throughout this journey but never realized how He was going to fulfill that promise. Slowly, I began to see that God was using cancer to bless me, and although I knew He was present in my heart, it was like a new realization that I was never alone. He constantly used circumstances, people, doctors, and strangers to show Himself to me. Surely, He is my refuge and strength.

This book is written to encourage and inspire others who are dealing with cancer or who have family members or friends with this disease. As I learned by journaling, the blessings of cancer far outweigh the days that I was so sick or experiencing pain. The title Experiencing The Blessings and Good Fruit of Cancer was chosen because of the blessings and variety of good fruit that cancer has produced in my own life. My challenge in each chapter is to encourage readers who have cancer to their open eyes and hearts to document the *Countless Blessings…the Lessons You Learn along the way…the ways to Improve your Self Esteem…the joy of learning how to become a Blessing to Others and finally, the Spiritual Growth that is a result of cancer.* If you are a family member or friend reading this book, it is my prayer that you will be challenged to discover ways to be a significant blessing to this special person in your life

Chapter 1

COUNTLESS BLESSINGS DURING CANCER

*BETTER TO LOSE COUNT WHILE NAMING
YOUR BLESSINGS THAN TO LOSE YOUR
BLESSINGS TO COUNTING YOUR TROUBLES.*
Maltble D. Babcock

INTRODUCTION

Blessings can be defined as bringing happiness or divine favor to an individual. I knew what blessings were because throughout my life I had received so many undeserved acts of kindness. However, when cancer invaded my life, it seemed as if the blessings were countless. Several weeks after breast surgery, I felt a strong need to keep a record of as many blessings as I could to remind me of how God was working in and through my life.

It is my desire to challenge those who are facing this disease to be willing to receive the blessings that God has in store for them. Some blessings will come through individuals, others will come in an experience where you know God is in control and yet, others will be when God speaks to you through His Word, a hymn, or a praise as you quietly suffer. Every blessing is a gift from God regardless of how or who delivers it.

On the following pages, I have shared examples of blessings that have lifted my spirit and blessed my life. As you read about my experiences, you may want to begin to make a list of blessings you have already received and give thanks for the person or situation that was instrumental in making them a part of your journey.

A wise man once said, "Learn to write your hurts
in sand and carve your blessings in stone."
unknown

THE BLESSING OF A MAMMOGRAM

Who would ever think that receiving a reminder to schedule your annual mammogram would be a blessing? The first reminder was discarded because I had convinced myself that no one in our family had ever had breast cancer, and since I had always received good reports, it would be okay to skip a year. However, a few weeks later, I received a second reminder and for some reason didn't discard it. I would look at it and conclude that it really was not necessary, but as the days passed, I realized that I was being foolish and their reminder was a means of helping me to stay on top of my health as a woman.

My appointment was scheduled on a Thursday and I'll never forget the nurse who did the mammogram telling me that she hoped that I didn't get a call to come back. Laughingly, I responded, "me too." However, early the next morning, I received a call telling me that they needed to schedule a follow up on Monday. Again I convinced myself that no one in our family had ever had breast cancer, so it had to be just a glitch.

The news following the sonogram was quite disturbing. I was told that the size and shape of the tumor indicated cancer, but a biopsy would be needed to confirm it. The biopsy confirmed their suspicion. Although my head was spinning with hearing the words "you have cancer", the doctor was already one step ahead of me. She had already called my primary doctor and they had a recommendation for a breast surgeon, who called me that afternoon and scheduled an appointment for the morning of Christmas Eve. What a blessing to have my husband and two daughters go with me for this consultation. It was amazing that all four of us knew beyond a shadow of a doubt that Dr. Bussey was the one to do the surgery which was scheduled for early February. Now, we could go home and celebrate Christmas!

**GLORY TO GOD IN THE HIGHEST
AND ON EARTH PEACE TO MEN ON
WHOM HIS FAVOR RESTS. Luke 2:14**

3

THE BLESSING OF FAMILY

A significant part of being diagnosed with cancer is allowing your family to walk this journey with you. My first impulse was to keep everything to myself and shelter them from worry; however, they reminded me that they were going to be with me every step of the way.

Angel Munoz, Kim Clayton, Lisa Stamey (deceased)
Wade and Judy Stamey

My loving husband of fifty three years assured me that cancer was just an illness and like every other challenge in life, we would get through it together. He became my greatest prayer warrior and as I listened to many of his prayers, tears of gratitude streamed down my face. The blessing of a Godly husband holding my hand through cancer makes each day a little better.

What a joy to have two daughters whose love and concern is expressed in so many ways. Their sacrifice of time from work and family has meant so much to me. Having two Godly daughters who know just what to say or do is a gift beyond measure. Our family was still grieving the loss of our oldest daughter, Lisa, who lost her battle with sarcoma cancer a year ago. Although she was an inspiration to us and "fought the good fight," we still struggle at trying to understand why she had to die so young. I remember her sisters, Kim and Angel, telling me that we needed to have a positive experience with cancer because we had had such a sad experience with Lisa's cancer. It reminded me that the loss of their sister and now the sudden knowledge that their mother had cancer was heavy on their hearts. It was important for me to be strong, keep a positive attitude, and pray that I would give them a positive experience, as well as a good example.

Another blessing is having a sister who faithfully prays for you and calls almost daily to let you know she loves you. Although a thousand miles separate us, she was faithful to send cards including a gift of money to help with meals following surgery and the chemo treatments.

The blessing of having four sisters-in-law who expressed their love and concern through their prayers, cards, calls, emails and gifts continues to be an inspiration. Each one always had the right words to say or offer the perfect scripture of encouragement for the day.

It's so important to keep in touch with your nieces, nephews, and cousins so they can be a part of your healing process. The blessings of having an extended family are incredible! Their notes, calls, cards, emails, and gifts have a special way of lifting your spirits. For example, one day I received two hand-made crocheted chemo hats from one of my cousins over a thousand miles away. God had touched her heart, and she was one step ahead of me. I had no idea that my bald head would get cold, and I would need a soft and warm covering. But more than that, she told me that every stitch was made with prayer.

When I reflect back to my thoughts of sheltering the family from my journey, I give thanks that God gave me wisdom to include them every step of the way. They have been a significant part of my healing process and ability to stay focused on the gift of life and the joy of family. It is important to allow those who love you to be a part of your life. Each one will respond differently, but I will assure you that each one will respond with the depth of love you need.

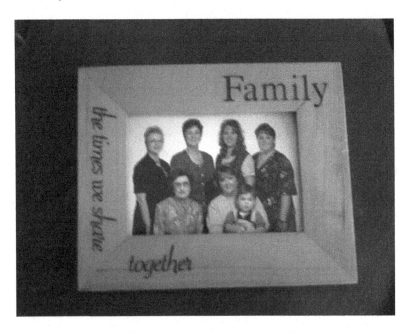

MAY YOU BE BLESSED BECAUSE YOU INCLUDED YOUR IMMEDIATE AND EXTENDED FAMILY ON YOUR JOURNEY WITH CANCER

THE BLESSING OF HAVING A CHURCH FAMILY

God loved us so much that He gave us the Holy Spirit, who lives within every believer, to provide comfort, direction, encouragement, and love. He is an ever present help throughout our earthly life. In addition to the gift of the Holy Spirit, God emphasized through his son, Jesus, the importance of believers coming together to worship, educate, evangelize, minister, and fellowship in a special place called the Church. As a believer and member of a church, we can experience each of these functions, but I want to focus on the importance of how I experienced the ministry of God's love from the church. It is my prayer that the following testimonies will encourage individuals who are suffering from the disease of cancer to actively seek the prayers and ministry of a local church.

My family was prepared for the early morning surgery. We had prayed and asked God's guidance of the surgeon's hands and success in removing the cancerous tumor. We believed I was in His care, but still there was anxiety about the unknown. After I had been prepared for surgery and was waiting on the doctor to arrive, we were blessed to receive a visit from our pastor and associate pastor. What a blessing to be encouraged and lifted up in prayer by our spiritual leaders. Following their visit, a special deacon from the church also came by to pray and offer a word of encouragement. Many times, people fail to let their church know about a crisis in their lives which means they will miss the prayers of other believers. I give thanks that my church wants to know of our needs so the leaders and members can engage in prayer on our behalf.

The church was faithful to pray for me and our family during the weeks of healing in preparation for the chemo treatments. In addition to the prayers, one member wanted me to know that she was going to bring dinner one day following my first chemo treatment. Because she was always so busy working and ministering to others, I was tempted to turn her offer down, but God reminded me that she wanted to minister to us and we happily accepted the meal with gratitude. She was an example of a familiar saying "The church gathers to worship and scatters to be Jesus in the world."

THE MINISTRY OF THE CROSSROADS BIBLE STUDY DEPARTMENT

On the Sunday before Chemo treatments began, the Director of our Sunday Morning Bible Study Department called and asked if it would be okay for the department to have a special prayer for me during the assembly time. I was grateful that they wanted to do this and agreed without hesitation. Prayer was my greatest need. Sunday morning arrived, and I looked forward to the outpouring of the love and prayers that would be offered on my behalf. Again, God is full of surprises. The department presented me with the most beautiful prayer quilt I had ever seen. Scripture verses were inscribed in many places, and again, each one of them had a special meaning in my life. When it was presented to me, I was reminded that each stitch was made with prayer, and the quilt would remind me that many people were praying that the cancer would be erased from my body and God would restore my health. The blessing of being a part of a church that cares is one of God's most precious gifts.

The dreaded day of chemo arrived on a rainy and gloomy day. However, we were blessed that the Oncology Center was only about a fifteen minute drive. The challenge of the unknown made me somewhat apprehensive, but we had prayed that things would go well and we could make it a positive experience. Again, God was actively working to answer our prayers. God blessed me with a Christian nurse who was heaven sent. She knew exactly what to say and do to make me feel at ease. There were many other nurses, but Debbie said it was okay for me to ask for her each time. She became a special part of my journey, and although we celebrated when I received the last treatment, it was bittersweet because I knew I would not see her again. I give thanks that God used her to bless my life, and He will continue to use her to bless others. However, this was just one of the blessings God had in store for me on this gloomy day. Although Debbie was not a member of the church I attended, she was an example of "the church scattered" by reflecting God's love through the many ways she ministered to me during each chemo treatment.

Another blessing occurred right after the chemo treatment began and within minutes, someone was knocking on the door to my room. An employee came in to deliver a beautiful gift that had been dropped off by a lady. I was quite puzzled because no one knew where I would be going for my treatments. Quickly, I opened the card and discovered that the gift was from a lady who was a member of my Bible Study class. We had just promoted into this class so I had not had the opportunity to get to know her. You can imagine how surprised I was that Pam had taken time to locate where I was having chemo and drove over twenty-five miles to bring me a gift of encouragement. Tears streamed down my face because the gift indicated that she knew me. Inside the package was a journal with the Bible verse "The Joy of the Lord is my Strength" on the cover plus bookmarkers that were inscribed with my favorite Bible verses of encouragement. I was blessed beyond measure that God had touched her life and called her to minister to me on this special day. It was amazing that this was just the beginning of a beautiful friendship. Pam walked along beside me all the way through the experience of chemo and radiation. I'll never forget the passion and love for Christ that overflowed and touched me in such a powerful way. In addition to her visits, phone calls, emails and cards, she either brought or sent a gift to me to open during my chemo treatments. I was overwhelmed with the generosity of time and precious gifts.

Weeks passed following my chemo treatments and when the time arrived to begin thirty-three radiation treatments, Pam was there to cheer me on. She had spent numerous hours preparing a gift she called "Radiation Inspiration." She had personally inscribed a card of inspiration and encouragement for each day.

The card I read today was entitled "Light". It said "a candle loses nothing by lighting another candle," followed by a personal note, "thank you, Judy for sharing the light of your life." As I read her words, I gave thanks for experiencing God's light through her life. The thirty three cards were truly inspired by God and she was a willing instrument of sharing His love and encouragement. What an example for me to follow!!! God has taught me so much through my new friend. I learned during our visits that Pam had suffered from cancer, not only once but twice and although the doctors still have to monitor her health, she has learned to live life to the fullest one day at a time. I am so grateful to be a member of the church where Pam and her husband John attend, worship and minister. What an inspiration and role model she continues to be in my life!

SUMMARY

One of the Fruits of Cancer is the Countless Blessings that can be overlooked if we allow ourselves to become obsessed by cancer and the unknowns it presents in our lives. The first thing the oncologist told me was that it was essential to have a positive attitude and focus on getting well rather than always thinking the worst or being negative about life. I was told that the patients who maintained a positive attitude made better progress. I was determined that even on the worst of days, I would listen to hymns, pray or have my husband read the Bible aloud as a means of keeping a positive attitude. Even when I was so sick I didn't have the strength to speak or communicate, it never failed that God's presence was evident and my thoughts of Him were comforting and merciful.

It is my prayer that you will be sensitive to the blessings that come into your life. Let these examples remind you that God is full of surprises and will bless you in ways that you least expect. Enjoy each one, give thanks, and make a note of it so you will remember and cherish each one. These memories will bless you immensely on the days that are most difficult.

**Every blessing is a gift from God regardless of
how or who delivers it.**

THE BLESSING OF FRIENDS AND NEIGHBORS

The anonymous quote "Friendship is love with wings" describes how I felt about each one who took time to minister to me and my family during this difficult time. When I think about the generosity of so many friends who took time to reach out to me with words of encouragement through phone calls, emails, cards, gifts and meals, I'm overwhelmed with thanksgiving. It is my desire to encourage you to lovingly accept the blessings from others. Although I cannot mentioned all the individuals who blessed me, I wanted to share several examples of how their actions reflected this quote.

Breast surgery was scheduled two days before Valentine's Day, which meant that my husband and I would celebrate it early this year. However, on Valentine's Day, Sandi and Beverly, two special ladies from our Bible Study class had planned a beautiful and delicious dinner for us. The tray was beautifully displayed with a gift along with a delicious stew, cornbread and special Valentine cookies. They made this day so special and we gave thanks as we celebrated our love and the love of friends. "Friendship is love with wings."

The doorbell rang and there was a man with a beautiful bouquet of flowers and I could hardly wait to open the card to see who had sent them. I stood there blessed because a committee of beautiful saints from Acton First Baptist Church in Granbury, Texas was reminding me of their love and prayers. It was my privilege to work with them as a church consultant and experience the love they had for the Lord and the church. Their act of encouragement brightened my day and lifted my spirits at a very difficult time in my life. "Friendship is love with wings."

Days before chemo began, I received a call from Donna and Johnny Sue, two special friends in Stephenville, who wanted to come to Fort Worth and take us to dinner. We happily accepted their invitation because it was always a joy and blessing to be with them on any occasion. I'll never forget how they made our time together so uplifting and positive, but most importantly, I'll never forget the prayers of these two women who lifted our names up to the Lord. We left that day agreeing that being with them was like sitting at the feet of Jesus. The beautiful part of this story is that their support and generosity has occurred many times throughout this journey, and each time has become more precious. "Friendship is love with wings."

On Friday before my first chemo treatment, I received a call from a young woman whom I had grown to admire. She is the daughter of one of the members of the senior adult group which I have led and traveled with for over thirty years. Jamie is a single parent who loves the Lord and strives to be an example of God's love to her children. In addition to that, she and her mother have such a loving and wonderful mother/daughter relationship. I wanted to describe Jamie to you because you can imagine my surprise when this young woman called to ask if she could come by and bring me a special coffee drink. She has so many responsibilities and lives over twenty miles away, but she wanted to take time out to bless me, and I was overjoyed that she would make this effort. In addition to a coffee drink, she arrived carrying a large bright pink basket filled to the brim and running over with gifts and special cards. I was speechless when she told me that her goal was for me to have a gift to open throughout the chemo treatments. It was her desire for me to have some bright spots along the way. God used her in a mighty way to touch my life with an overflowing of His love. Every gift was perfectly planned and blessed me throughout this difficult journey in a way that I'll never forget. "Friendship is love with wings."

When Jesus talks about loving your neighbor, I immediately think of Simone who has been our next door neighbor for over forty years. Since her husband went to be with the Lord, we have become especially close and when I told her about my cancer, she immediately began to pray for me. In the days that followed, she brought me a beautiful card from her priest indicating that her church was also praying for me. However, her concern did not stop there; she faithfully brought a full meal to the house the day after each chemo treatment in addition to other special gifts. What a blessing!!! "Friendship is love with wings."

What a joy I have had for over thirty years to work with "The Young at Heart", a group of senior adults who love the Lord and still want to fellowship and travel together. The majority of them joined the group when they were in their sixties and now most of them are in their eighties and nineties, which means they are limited in the ways they can minister to one another. The ministry of prayer is a significant gift; however, they wanted to add to it by showering us with gift cards we could use for meals. They also remembered me with several gift cards from Starbucks, a special treat for Wade and me. Age may limit what you can do, but there are still ways to bless others. "Friendship is love with wings."

Another young woman whom God has brought into my life is Sheila. She is also a single mom who works with Jamie and wanted to travel with the Young at Heart on several of our adventures. Her love for the Lord was evident from the first time we met. I was thrilled that she and Jamie wanted to travel with an older group of people. They were a blessing to everyone. However, I hesitated to share with Sheila that I had cancer because of my concern that it would remind her of the recent years when she walked alongside her sister who had recently died from breast cancer. It had been such a painful experience for her as she ministered to her during her last days. Sheila faithfully sent me cards of encouragement, but then one day she called and asked if she could come by after work. I'll never forget her visit. She was full of encouragement, and her thoughtfulness included bringing a gift of things I needed for a manicure and pedicure. Her experience with her sister enabled her to share with me things that would be helpful especially as I began the chemo treatments. What a God sent messenger and friend! "Friendship is love with wings."

The phone rang and when I answered it, I quickly discovered it was one of my students who attended the certification program I directed at the Southwestern Certification Center. He had heard that I was encountering cancer and told me that he wanted to come over to visit me. I knew he served in a mega church in Dallas and his schedule was always full, but ironically, he didn't ask if he could come, he asked when he could come. Daryl made me feel so special when he asked what would be a good time to come and then he insisted on bringing a meal. Over forty miles away, God had touched the heart of this busy minister to come to Fort Worth and minister to us. His visit was as if the Lord had walked into our home with a meal, words of encouragement, and a prayer that touched our heart and soul. Daryl's son, Joshua, was with him and before they left, they gave each of us a special coin engraved with the armor of Christ and a reminder to pray always. "Friendship is love with wings."

Lastly, the chemo treatments had been very difficult and I was limited on what I could do, so one of the highlights of the day was getting the mail. Hardly a day passed without a card or note of encouragement, and most of the time, I would cry tears of gratitude that so many people cared for me and were praying for my recovery. One day, there was a brown envelope from Houston. I eagerly opened it to find a beautiful scarf from Peggy, one of my certification students, who knew that I could dress up a cap or hat with it. I was overcome with gratitude that God had touched her heart to bless me and go out of her way to minister to me. "Friendship is love with wings."

Friendship Is Love With Wings

In summary, these are only a few examples which can remind us of how important it is to be available to receive God's blessings and enjoy the surprises of the people He chooses to be His messengers. We must learn to humble ourselves and give thanks that God is with us and many times comes in the flesh to bless us.

Chapter 2

LESSONS LEARNED FROM CANCER

INTRODUCTION

Cancer has become a teacher and I discovered that I am the pupil. One would think that the lessons of cancer would be depressing and sad; however, I have been amazed by the positive impact they have made on my life. The lessons were valuable sources of instruction, inspiration, and encouragement.

I would like to share five lessons that have had a special meaning in my life. It is my desire that they will encourage and inspire others in similar situations to seek and learn from this difficult time in their lives.

LESSON ONE: SELF CENTERED THOUGHTS DISPELLED

It is so easy to get caught up in centering all our thoughts around our cancer and lose sight of what others around us are going through. God was quick to remind me that there were many other people who were suffering with an illness or disease which is considered much greater than my breast cancer. God allowed people to cross my path who had just received transplants and were in great danger of their bodies rejecting it, some who had rare diseases where scientists and doctors had not found a cure, and still others who had been given a short time to live.

The first lesson I learned from my cancer was that I needed to be more vigilant as a vessel of encouragement and let each person I encountered know that I am praying for them. The scripture "let your light shine before others, that they may see your good deeds and glorify your Father in heaven" (Matt. 5:16) challenged me to see beyond myself.

LESSON TWO: WHY ME? WHY NOT ME?

Our daughter Lisa, who died from sarcoma cancer of the scalp, taught me many valuable lessons which have been reinforced in my own life. When she was told that the kind of cancer she had was terminal and had only about five months to live, she said "Mom, you never ask God 'why me?', you ask 'why not me?'" What a valuable lesson to learn. It changes your perspective and allows God to use you to bless others with hope and encouragement as long as you live.

Another important quote Lisa shared with me many times continues to teach me as I walk on this journey. It went like this, "Life isn't about waiting for the storm to pass...it's about learning to dance in the rain." This was a statement she made many times as her dad and I watched her battle a rare and horrible cancer. She modeled dancing in the rain through her faith in God, her smile, her positive attitude and encouragement to us. This quote and her example have been a significant part of my journey. Although I felt that my faith in God was strong, it was often difficult to maintain a positive attitude, to keep a smile on my face and to actively encourage others while suffering from the side effects of chemo. However, with God's help, I believe I have been able to learn how to dance in the rain and hopefully have been a good example to my children and others.

LESSON THREE: FOLLOWING INSTRUCTIONS

I learned the hard way that when the oncologist or surgeon gives you instructions, it's essential to listen carefully and understand that they are looking out for your best interest. Dr. Richey emphasized the importance of calling day or night if I had a fever of 100.4 or higher. However, it was four o'clock on a Saturday morning when I was awakened with a fever of 101, and because it was the weekend, I decided not to call the doctor. Coping with the fever went on until Monday morning, at which time, I called his office and was told that it was important for me to come in to get help right away. They immediately administered fluids for dehydration and antibiotics for infections. The nurse told me that I was one of the fortunate ones because fever usually indicated a serious infection and getting help should not be delayed. She reminded me that a 100.4 fever was a result of research and emphasized the importance of calling the doctor immediately.

LESSON FOUR: NO HAIR? BALD?

When I heard the oncologist say that my hair would probably begin to come out ten days following my first chemo treatment, I convinced myself that this would not happen to me. I was so proud of my hair because the older I got, the darker my hair would get. This was a trait I received from my parents and how I loved saying that I didn't have to color my hair.

However, weeks before my first chemo treatment, Mary, my hair stylist, encouraged me to purchase a wig while I still had hair. She said choosing the right color would make the wig look more natural. Because she had several clients with cancer and styled their wigs, she was able to refer me to an excellent wig shop. Although I thought I may not need one, I followed her suggestion and was fitted with a wig that she styled exactly like my hair. Having a wig that looked so much like my natural hair gave me peace of mind that **IF** I lost my hair, I was ready.

Ten days passed, none of my hair had come out, and I was getting excited; however, five days later, it happened! My excitement faded as I realized that I was going to lose my hair. Each day I lost a little more and finally accepted the realization that I would soon be bald. It was important to me that I make this a positive experience. Therefore, I decided that it was time to shop for caps so I wouldn't have to wear a wig all the time. In addition to shopping, I went to the American Cancer Society office where I was given another wig, several caps, and various head pieces. I was so impressed with their generosity and encouragement.

Finally, the day came when I was totally bald and saw myself in the mirror for the first time without hair. It was an eye opening experience! First of all, I was reminded of how my deceased daughter and I looked so much alike and how much I missed seeing her smiling face. Secondly, I was reminded that Lisa was not as fortunate as her Mom. The radiation treatments on her head meant that if she had lived, she would never have grown hair again, but I was more fortunate because my hair would grow back in about eight to ten months.

Baldness reinforced my mother's words,
"Beauty is only skin deep,
and true beauty comes from the inside out."

LESSON FIVE: INTIMACY WITH MY HUSBAND

**Judy and Wade
celebrating 50th Anniversary in Hawaii**

I was so fearful breast cancer was going to affect the great relationship I had with my husband. Would the surgery, treatments, and medications take away my desire to express my love and enjoy sex? How would my husband respond to having a bald headed wife? These were major questions that needed to be addressed, and it was important that I discuss my concerns with him.

How would my husband of fifty two years feel about seeing me bald, especially in bed? I was scared that he would see me differently, because I was convinced that I would see myself differently. However, my concern was in vain. He reminded me that I would be beautiful to him with or without hair. From the very first day of baldness, he would rub my head lovingly and call me "baby". His affectionate title became a source of fun for us and I would often surprise him by wearing a cute headband to bed. I am so grateful that love is blind and when he tells me I am beautiful, I believe him.

Another concern was related to how the treatments and medications would affect our intimacy. When I began this discussion with my husband, he told me that the most important thing was my recovery and he knew our love would grow even deeper throughout this experience. However, when I expressed my concern about losing the intimacy we enjoyed, he was quick to tell me that it may be limited, but we would still enjoy the kisses, hugs, hand holding, and just being together. My sweet husband assured me that there would be "sex after breast cancer," and we would know when the time was right for this expression. I was thankful that there were days throughout the treatments that we enjoyed the gift of sex and were able to forget about the bad days caused by cancer.

SUMMARY

A person does not have a choice about whether or not they will encounter the horrible disease we call "cancer." It comes when we least expect it and challenges us in many ways. The tests, surgeries, treatments and medications become a part of our lives for many months or even years. We may not have a choice about how our cancer is treated, but we have a choice about how we will respond to it. May I suggest that in addition to observing the blessings we receive from cancer as described in chapter one, it is also important to document some of the important lessons we learn as we travel on this journey. Our learning experiences may be helpful to someone else who is experiencing a similar illness.

Chapter 3

SELF ESTEEM ISSUES DURING CANCER

INTRODUCTION

Self esteem is critical to one's emotional and psychological health. It is the image we have of ourselves that has grown out of a lifetime of experiences. A person with poor self esteem tends to focus on the present and seeks affirmation to counteract negative thoughts of self worth and value. On the other hand, a person who has good self esteem accepts themselves, warts and all. They recognize their abilities and failures and chose not to allow the disappointments in life to destroy their positive self image and self respect. One of the greatest commandments Jesus gave us was "to love our neighbor as we love ourselves" (Mark 12:31). The first time I really understood what He was saying, I was in my thirties and trying to be a perfect wife, mother, seminary student, minister, and friend. My zeal for perfection in every area of my life led to stress and frustration. When I realized that in my quest to make everyone else happy, I was not happy with myself. It was evident that my self esteem was very poor and I was crying out for affirmation from those who surrounded my life. Through a series of books, the Bible, and Christian counseling, I discovered that I was a person of worth and God loved me in times of success as well as in times of failure. As my self esteem improved, it became clearer to me that it is almost impossible to truly love another if we do not love and respect ourselves. Maintaining a healthy self esteem is probably one of my greatest challenges, but I give thanks to God for reminding me throughout His Word that we are created in His image, and I am a person of value and worth.

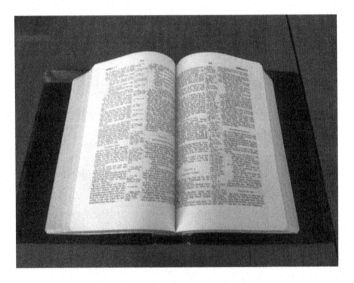

Your word is a lamp for my feet, a light
on my path. Psalm 119:105

It is not unusual for a person's self esteem to fluctuate from time to time. Life is full of ups and downs which will cause us to question our worth or ability to be successful in various situations. However, the person with a healthy self esteem will experience only temporary setbacks because they know how they really feel about themselves. On the other hand, a person with poor self esteem tends to allow setbacks to linger much longer which can drastically affect their relationships and ability to make good decisions. Therefore, it is essential for a person diagnosed with cancer to accept the disease as a physical challenge and not allow it to damage their self esteem or drastically affect how they see themselves.

This advice is much easier to say than it is to do. Your head is spinning with all the information the doctor has given you about the treatments, what you are to expect, plus describing all the side effects you may encounter. The last thing you want to think about is having a healthy self esteem. However, I believe as soon as the shock of cancer is accepted, we must look ourselves in the mirror and remind ourselves that we are special and choose to live each day to the best of our ability. I also think that it is important for us to make a commitment to be an advocate of positive and healthy thoughts.

The following examples are challenges I have faced on my journey with cancer. Hopefully they will be helpful to you as you seek to maintain a healthy self esteem.

SELF ESTEEM AND OUR INNER CRITIC

People compliment us or offer words of concern, but too often our inner critic begins to question what they said or how they said it. Sometimes, we convince ourselves that they just felt obligated to say something nice, and they just feel sorry for us. Instead of listening to your inner critic, accept the compliment and words of concern or encouragement as a gift and thank God that He has placed people in your life that care enough to say something.

SELF ESTEEM AND BEING KIND TO YOURSELF

Sometimes we are our own worst critic. It is important to treat yourself the way you would treat a friend who has cancer. Be kind and encourage yourself as you begin the journey of cancer. One of the ways I encouraged myself was by planning ahead. I realized that there was the likelihood that following chemo I would spend more time in bed, so I shopped for pretty new sheets, which turned out to be a great gift to myself. Treating yourself with kindness is one way to improve your self esteem and will make a significant contribution to your healing process. Another thing I did was to enjoy some of my favorite foods the week before the first chemo treatment. I was so glad I did because my taste buds changed and it was weeks after the last treatment before the taste of many foods returned.

SELF ESTEEM AND LOOKS

A person's internal mirror is much more important than the outside mirror we use to evaluate our appearances. As a mother, it was important for me to be an example to my daughters and teach them that "beauty is only skin deep" and true beauty comes from within and will last forever. It was essential to communicate to them that Christian beauty produces a smile that is unquestionably real and a radiance that reflects God's love and blesses others. Although beauty is only skin deep, I believe that when a Christian is physically well kept, including taking care of her hair, nails, make-up, and wearing modest outer garments, she will bless more people and influence them in a positive way.

The side effects of cancer were going to be an appearance challenge. I never felt like I was naturally pretty, so it was important to me to have a hairstyle I could take care of and never leave home without some make-up on and looking presentable. However, things were about to change. How would I prepare to go out in public without hair, eye brows, or eye lashes?

The quote "First impressions are lasting impressions" has guided me most of my life. As a minister and public speaker, I was keenly aware that one's appearance was a significant contributor to credibility and I may not have another opportunity to meet these individuals again. The affects cancer would have upon my looks encouraged me to seek ways that I could continue to look my best.

First of all, when I went to purchase a wig, the lady was so helpful. As a former employee of the American Cancer Society in Fort Worth, her expertise on head coverings and make-up tips was just what I needed. She encouraged me to always look my best as a gift to myself, emphasizing how it would make me feel better.

Another thing I did was to purchase cute hats, caps, and glitzy jewelry. It was fun to match up outfits with the different items. One of my favorite things was to wear large earrings and rings on my fingers. It was amazing how many people would compliment me on the accessories, which helped me forget for a little while about my altered looks.

In addition to hair pieces and glitzy jewelry, it was important for me to keep my nails looking good with manicures and pedicures. I was fortunate that my daughter, Angel, who lived nearby, would do this for me when I didn't feel like doing it myself or going out to have it done.

Looks are important to our well being and I'm grateful for the many simple ways that I have been able to make myself look presentable. It is also important to remember that chemo and other medications dehydrate the skin; therefore, moisturizers are essential to keeping a healthy looking face.

AND HEAVENS, DON'T FORGET THE LIPSTICK!!!

Chapter 4

HOW CANCER CAN BLESS OTHERS

INTRODUCTION

> "Life is not about receiving at all times; it is a
> combination of being thankful for what you have
> as blessings and sharing those blessings with others
> who need a little fraction of what you have."
> *Catherine Pulsifer, Moms Wisdom*

This quote continues to challenge me as I reflect upon the blessings that have been bestowed upon me throughout the cancer journey. Every time I received a blessing or act of kindness, my heart would overflow with gratitude and yet, I was humbled knowing that I was so undeserving of these kindnesses. The question I kept asking myself was "How could I be a blessing to someone else while suffering through chemo treatments and radiation?" I didn't want to wait until I felt better or was cancer free to help someone else who was in need. I wanted to touch others with the same kind of love and compassion that God placed in the hearts of others to help me get through this difficult time.

Another challenge was the advice I continually received from others. They would say "you must put yourself first now and forget doing for others until you are well." Although I knew that this advice was coming from loving hearts, I could not let this type of thinking penetrate into my heart. I understood the importance of taking care of myself and doing what the doctor said, but to forget doing for others was not an option. Therefore, I asked God to impress upon my heart the things I could do to bless others in the midst of my trials with cancer. He was faithful to give me opportunities to serve Him and bless others all along the way. However, let me be quick to say that every time I thought God was using me to bless someone else, I was the one who received a blessing.

Cancer may limit us in many ways, but it also opens the door to be a blessing to others. I want to share with you how God used my cancer to serve and bless others. As you read about my experiences, it is my prayer that you will determine how God can use you to bless others regardless of your circumstances.

POPCORN MINISTRY

Wade and I are volunteers at Baylor All Saints Hospital where we make and sell popcorn on Wednesdays. We were concerned about being able to continue our service during the chemo treatments, but since my chemo was administered on Tuesdays and I did not get sick until Thursdays, we did not have to miss a day. Making and selling popcorn is a ministry that we take very seriously. Every customer is either visiting a loved one, coming for treatment, or is employed by the hospital. Although our visits with customers may be brief, we always have the opportunity to pass on a smile and words of encouragement which often leads to being told how we can pray for them. I was surprised and amazed at how God was going to use my cancer to expand this ministry. When someone shared they were there with a loved one who was being treated for cancer or had just been diagnosed themselves with cancer, it opened the door even wider for God to use me to encourage them and pass on my faith. As a result, many of them would come back every Wednesday to buy popcorn, but more than that, to share an update or prayer request.

I'll never forget one man who came every Wednesday for many weeks to buy popcorn. We discovered that his wife was critically ill and in addition to his popcorn, he needed someone to talk to about their journey. We were so glad to be there to listen, encourage, and offer our prayers for both of them. One day as he walked away, he turned around and came back to hand me a twenty dollar bill with these words, "I know this is not a lot, I wish it were a thousand dollars, but you and your husband have blessed me so much each week that I want to give this as a token of appreciation." I thanked him and let him know that his donation would mean a great deal to many people because all the popcorn income was used by the Auxiliary to provide funds for research and other ministry needs in the hospital.

One day, I took a break from the popcorn station to go to the ladies room to remove my cap and wipe the sweat off my bald head. There were only two stalls in the room and I didn't see anyone around so I took my cap off and said aloud to myself "Judy, you are not pretty at all today." To my surprise, a young lady immediately came out of the stall and looked at me with the most beautiful brown eyes and said, "Ma'am, I heard what you said and you are wrong, you are beautiful." This started a conversation that led her to tell me about some decisions she had to make regarding the high possibility of her getting cancer before she was thirty. After an extended time of listening and encouraging her, I'll never forget her response. She hugged me and proceeded to tell me that our meeting was not by chance, it was Divine Providence, and she was blessed. I walked away thanking God for the unexpected blessing I received, but more than that, I thanked Him for using my cancer to open a door to bless her.

Another way God inspired us to be a blessing to someone was when a young man came by the popcorn machine and handed us several dollars requesting that we use it to pay for the next person who came to buy popcorn. This was a perfect example of giving forward, and we had such joy in seeing the gratitude on the face of the one who received his generosity that we decided we would bring extra money each week so we could do the same thing. To tell a mom who's looking for change in her purse that we'd be honored to buy her child a box of popcorn is a priceless experience. This has opened doors of conversation that God has used to bless both the receiver and the giver.

What a blessing that God can take one of the most difficult times in our lives and use it to bless others even while selling popcorn. It's important to stay alert and be available to bring a ray of sunshine into another life even when you have a dark cloud hanging over your own life. It's amazing that as we bless others, our dark cloud seems to get a little lighter.

VOCATIONAL MINISTRY

Many people who deal with cancer must also deal with going to work each day. The side effects of cancer often make it difficult to produce at the same level as you did before treatments began. Although I did not have a regular job to go to, I continued to serve as a church consultant, which included speaking engagements, on campus consulting and evaluating church documents. God had given me assignments, which I took very seriously long before I was diagnosed with cancer and I simply refused to cancel them. I knew I wasn't indispensable but believed that God had a reason for each one of them. As I share with you one example of how God used me to keep my commitment, I hope you will see how He used my journey with cancer to inspire and bless someone else through my work.

Last fall, I accepted an assignment to speak to a group of church administrators at a breakfast meeting provided by the PSK Accounting Firm in Arlington, Texas. The topic I had chosen was entitled "Spring will Come," meaning that we all go through the winters of life where the trials and challenges seem like they will last forever, but we must hold on because Spring will come.

Spring Will Come!!!

However, at the time that I gave them the topic, I didn't realize that I would be experiencing one of the worst winters of my life. In addition, I found out my first chemo treatment would be on Tuesday and the breakfast was only two days away. I became concerned about my ability to keep my commitment. After much prayer and with my husband's encouragement, I knew I did not need to cancel this engagement. Thursday morning came early. One of the side effects of my treatment was the inability to sleep, which hit me about one o'clock in the morning. At three thirty, I prayed that God would allow me at least a couple of hours of sleep; my prayer was answered, and I woke up at five thirty ready to keep my commitment.

Over and over again I prayed that God would use this engagement to bless at least one administrator with encouragement and hope. Because of the fear of becoming emotional, I had asked that during the introduction they would not mention my cancer.

This enabled me to keep my focus on the mission I had been given. Although I did not feel my physical best, I felt that God was speaking through me and enabled me to communicate with the group. The attendees were very affirmative and expressed appreciation for the encouragement; be that as it may, it is always difficult to determine how it had truly impacted their lives. However, God sent His affirmation through the mail.

I received a letter a week later stating that God had used me to bless one of the participants in a special way, and that meant the world to me. Let me share an excerpt from the letter, which may express what someone else may be saying about you.

...I want you to know what an impact you've made on me. More importantly than the words you spoke was the way in which you spoke them. I can honestly say that the glory of God radiates from you...The first time I heard you speak you were going through the winter season of losing your daughter. This time, you are facing a serious illness. Somehow through it all, your face and your smile radiate spring. You are really an inspiration and I wanted you to know.

This is a reminder that our testimony is more than words. It is only when our words are honest and sincere that God can use them to bless others. In addition, it is a reminder of the power of our face, especially when we can smile even in the midst of winter. I challenge you to bless others with words of encouragement and smiles of hope. You may never know how God is using you, but trust that He is working through every encounter at home, at school, at work, at church and at play.

RELAY FOR LIFE MINISTRY

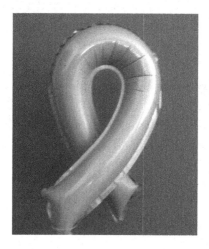

Our daughter Kim, who lives in Sachse, Texas, became a team leader for the Relay for Life Event in Garland when her sister was diagnosed with sarcoma cancer of the scalp. She takes her role as a leader very seriously, and through her website and other means, she has been able to reach her contribution goal each year. Although Lisa passed away in 2011, Kim has continued her mission of helping the American Cancer Society to find a cure for cancer.

This year Kim insisted that I be a part of the Survivor Walk and that her dad walk beside me as my Caregiver. This was very difficult to do since I was in the middle of chemo treatments. However, we wanted to please our daughter and we began the walk, which was quite a moving experience. The presence of God was evident as we heard people talking about how long they had survived. As I neared the end of the lap, a lady in a golf cart noticed that I was getting short winded and stopped to pick me up. She insisted and proceeded to take us to the Survivor's Dinner which was provided by various restaurants in the area. At this time, I didn't realize what God was doing, but when we arrived at the tent, we were seated across from a young woman who later told me she was thirty-three years old and was celebrating being cancer free. God had planned our seating and for the next hour we were given the opportunity to minister to her and her husband with encouragement and prayer. We left the dinner table thanking God for this opportunity and for the special blessing we received from them.

Again, I discovered that opportunities to bless others often come when least expected and we must be available to give and be a blessing.

SUMMARY

How easy it would be to allow cancer to stop your life because of the fear, but this does not need to happen. I shared these examples believing God wanted to use me to bless and encourage others to continue to live, even though it may be in moderation. I have learned that every chemo treatment had a similar, but different response; therefore, learning to live one day at a time was essential. You may have to postpone something you had planned, but wait a few days and then proceed with living. It is often through God using us to bless others that we receive some of our greatest blessings.

> *When I am afraid, I put my trust in you. Psalm 56:3*

Chapter 5

SPIRITUAL GROWTH THROUGH CANCER

INTRODUCTION

> "...bearing fruit in every good work, growing
> in the knowledge of God...."
> Col 1:10b

Many times we question God's presence when we face the trials of life. In the midst of pain and suffering, it is easy to feel all alone. It was important for me to look back at my walk with the Lord and remember how He had never left me or forsaken me during my times of need. I claimed this promise on the day that I asked Jesus Christ to come into my life as Lord and Savior, and I give thanks for the assurance that He is an ever present help.

Throughout life's most difficult situations, His presence has given me peace that passes all understanding plus the strength and courage for each new day. As I looked back at all the challenges I have encountered in life, I was overwhelmed with how He revealed Himself to me in every situation. Most recently, I recalled the strength, love and wisdom He bestowed upon Wade and me as we walked through the illness and death of our daughter. This was the most difficult time we had ever faced. However, as difficult as it was for us to see our daughter die, God held us close and gave us the strength, comfort and the ability to thank Him for allowing Lisa to be a part of our family for forty eight years. His presence and how He has sustained us will remain a mystery until we meet Him face to face. Following Lisa's death, we have continually prayed for our faith to increase and our lives to touch others with His love. As result of Lisa's battle with cancer, our spiritual lives were challenged to draw closer to our Lord. We needed Him more than ever!

It was only fifteen months after Lisa's death when I found out I had cancer. My first concern was thinking about how my husband and daughters were going to accept another battle with cancer. Would they be mad at God or question their faith? It was at that point I realized how important it was for me to be a Godly wife and mother who would be there to help them through another difficult time.

OVERCOMING FEAR

> "I sought the Lord, and he answered me;
> he delivered me from all my fears." Psalm 34:4

Fear can be a powerful force that can paralyze our ability to move forward. I knew this and had spent my life encouraging others to give their fears to the Lord and trust Him to work through every situation. However, the fear of having an aggressive cancer challenged me with thoughts of "what if" as well as planning my memorial service. Then I realized that Satan was trying to distract me from the promises of God with negative thoughts and lack of trust. It was at this point that I cried out to the Lord and asked

Him to replace my fears with faith and trust that would result in bringing glory to Him.

Fear never walks very far from us and I remember how quickly it returned when I was told that the port surgery had not been successful. When I returned to the hospital to correct the procedure, I was overcome with fear. The doctor who had put it in had turned it over to another doctor and there was some confusion over what they were going to do. As I lay on the table waiting, I began to quote scripture and pray that God would guide their hands so there would be no further complications. The peace that overcame me was unmistakably the presence of the Lord. He banished the fear and replaced it with peace.

God understands how fear can creep into our lives. All throughout scripture, God instructs us not to fear. I knew this was going to be a great challenge for me, but then I remembered how Peter's faith enabled him to walk on water until he became afraid of the boisterous winds and began to sink. Peter's experience challenged me to keep my eyes on Jesus, trusting him to be there every step of the way. Because I knew God was victorious over fear, I was not going to allow the fear of cancer to paralyze and keep me from doing God's will.

But when he saw the wind, he was afraid and, beginning to sink, cried out, "Lord, save me!" Immediately Jesus reached out his hand, and caught him. "You of little faith," he said, "why did you doubt?" Matt 14: 30-31

PERSONAL BIBLE STUDY AND PRAYER

Everyday for many years, Wade and I begin each day with reading the Bible and praying together. It's been amazing how God speaks to us each day and even though we've read the Word through for seven years, He continually opens our eyes and hearts to specific truths we need for the day. The Bible is truly the living Word of God!

There were many days I could not participate in our Bible reading by reading aloud the portion I usually read, but Wade would read it for me. Sometimes my eyes would not focus, but my ears were eager to hear what God's Word was for the day. It's hard to explain how God gave me strength, even when physically I had no strength to read or get out of bed.

My prayer for others with cancer is to make daily Bible reading and prayer a priority. This is absolutely the greatest gift God has given to us. In case there's no one to read to you during those difficult days, you can install a free Bible on your IPad or computer that will read it aloud to you.

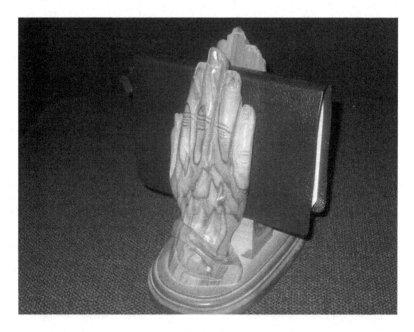

> *Your word is a lamp for my feet, a light*
> *on my path. Psalm 119:105*

CORPORATE WORSHIP AND SMALL GROUP INVOLVEMENT

Although going to church to worship had always been a priority in our lives, when I found out I had cancer, it became more important than ever. I didn't want to miss praising God and hearing the message He was going to speak to me through the pastor. On the days I wasn't well enough to go to church, I would worship with television preachers.

Small group involvement was an absolute! Our Bible study department and class provided an arena of God's love and corporate prayer. Even when I could not be there, I was assured of their ongoing prayers. In addition to their ministry of prayer, the teacher would challenge us through God's Word with a special nugget of truth I needed to hear.

My prayer for each person with cancer is that they will make their church family a part of the journey. One way I was able to do this was by keeping them informed through periodic email updates listing specific prayer concerns and requests. Although you may never know who or how many people are praying, it is a great comfort to know that people are lifting your name to the Lord.

MINISTERING TO OTHERS

When you find out you have cancer, it is the beginning of a journey that seems like a time for you to take a "time out" from serving others; however, I discovered the opposite. Doing for others in the midst of a serious illness became a blessing that lifted my spirits and increased my desire to get well. A disease that could be terminal reminded me of Jesus' second greatest commandment to love our neighbor as ourselves.

> "Love the Lord your God with all your
> heart and with all your soul and with all
> your mind and with all your strength.
> The second is this: 'Love your neighbor as yourself.'
>
> There is no commandment greater than these."
>
> Mark 12:30-31

People mean well when they tell you to put your life on hold and take care of yourself. However, when we turn our thoughts inward, we are running the risk of becoming depressed or self centered. It is important to recognize that in the midst of treatments, there will be some good days when we can choose to be a blessing to someone else. I believe that serving others is a significant part of the healing process.

INCREASED FAITH AND TRUST IN GOD

I was nine years old when I trusted my life to Jesus and asked Him into my heart. Trusting God was easy because my parents and grandparents modeled trusting Him with everything, and I knew that He had never failed them. My faith and trust in God continued to grow during my youth and young adult years; however, the older I get, I realize, more than ever, that God wants to be a part of every aspect of my life. So many times, when I didn't have a clue about what or how to pray about a situation, I would just ask God for His will to be done and give me strength to accept it. And that's exactly how I felt the day I was told I had cancer. I didn't know how to pray, so I asked God to give me the strength and wisdom to accept the cancer and use it to glorify

Him, whether in life or in death. From that day forward, I could face whatever confronted me.

One of my favorite Bible passages is from Proverbs 3:5-6 NLT "Trust in the LORD with all your heart; do not depend on your own understanding; seek His will in all you do, and He will show you which path to take." This promise has kept me from wavering and worrying about the tomorrows and helped me to stay focused on today making it the "best day of the rest of my life."

BOLD WITNESS FOR CHRIST

Witnessing for Christ has been a part of my life since becoming a Christian. I have participated in many witnessing training classes designed to give me the tools to be a more effective witness. However, when I began to deal with all the ramifications of cancer, it became evident God was using it to open doors for me to give a "bold witness" to doctors, other patients, and people in places where I shopped and traveled. It is such a blessing to be able to turn the conversations about my cancer into how God has blessed our lives through this disease. The joy of sharing Christ and his good works with others is a rewarding part of cancer.

For I am not ashamed of this Good News about Christ. It is the power of God at work, saving everyone who believes the Jew first and also the Gentile. This Good News tells us how God makes us right in his sight. This is accomplished from start to finish by faith. As the Scriptures say, "It is through faith that a righteous person has life."
Romans 1:16-17 NLT

SUMMARY

These are some of the most significant ways that cancer has been a part of my spiritual growth. The older I get and the longer I walk with the Lord, I realize my spiritual immaturity and the need to examine my life for evidence of how God's love is touching the lives of others. I'm thankful that He is using cancer to draw me closer to Him and challenging me to "let others see Jesus in me."

CONCLUSION

Thank you for investing your time to read about my journey with breast cancer. Each page was written with a prayer that my experience would inspire and encourage you to look for the good that comes from cancer with an emphasis on allowing others to be a part of your journey.

I acknowledge that my battle with cancer was definitely a battle. I was not exempt from pain, fever, loss of sleep, fatigue, and other side effects that are most common with chemo and radiation treatments. However, I was keenly aware of the importance of maintaining a positive attitude and recognizing that at my lowest point, the sun would shine again. I am praying that you will work hard to keep a positive attitude and God willing you will see the sunshine much quicker than I did.

Breast cancer has required almost a year of my life for doctor appointments and treatments, presenting quite a challenge to live a normal life. However, all of my doctors advised me of the importance of doing everything I could to live as normal as possible and they were committed to work with me on appointments and treatments. I was so blessed that each one helped me so that I did not have to cancel a vacation or speaking engagement and still got quality care. Normal is somewhat of an exaggeration because throughout this chapter of our lives, we do not feel our best. The fatigue that results from the chemo continues to linger long after the treatments are complete; therefore, it is important to make resting the body a priority as needed. However, in light of this, remember to participate and enjoy the company of others or special activities as much as possible.

Again, may I challenge you to keep a journal of

> *blessings you receive during your cancer journey*
> *lessons you learn from your cancer journey*
> *ways you are keeping your self esteem healthy in spite of the physical challenges*
> *how you are blessing others in the midst of fighting cancer*
> *ways your relationship with God is growing throughout the cancer challenge*

OH NO!!! NOT AGAIN

My heart sank when the doctor confirmed that my wife had breast cancer. It had been only fifteen months ago that our daughter lost her battle with sarcoma cancer of the scalp. We were still grieving and now we were facing a new battle with cancer. During the three year illness of our daughter, we drew strength from one another as we ministered to her. This time our roles were changing. I would become the caretaker, who would love, encourage and be there to help Judy each step of the way. Looking back, I give thanks that God gave me wisdom to know what to do, an overflowing of love and patience which meant I could sit quietly by her bed for days and pray for her as she suffered from the chemo treatments. Even though it was not my body, cancer had become a real part of my life and when she hurt, I hurt too. Judy's love and gratitude were ever present and I give thanks that we refused to let cancer control our lives. It was a long battle, but in the midst of the battle, God provided strength, promises and love that resulted in victory every day.

Wade Stamey, Husband, Friend, Sweetheart

Cancer is probably the most dreaded word a person would want to hear, yet Judy and Wade turned this disease that took their daughter Lisa's life into a witness for Christ. Their faith was evident in word, action and demeanor. Every time I thought of them and their courageous fight, Judy's often quoted scripture, "the joy of the Lord is my strength" popped into my head. Not knowing Judy and Wade personally at that time, my only connection to them was praying for Lisa and their family. Later, Judy and Wade became a part of my Bible Study Class, and it was then I learned she had breast cancer. Having had breast cancer and what the doctors believed to have been ovarian cancer within a period of two years, I immediately identified with Judy and thought "I must do for her what others did for me." The Golden Rule was one of the first things learned as a child, and I have tried always to put myself in someone else's place. So there is no doubt in my mind or heart that God spoke to me and wanted me to put my faith into action; therefore, I made plans to give Judy a gift for each chemo treatment remembering my excitement as I opened gifts from my children before not only one but two, actually three, chemo cycles! My children said to tell the oncologist, "No more chemo, we are running out of ideas!" In addition to the chemo gifts, my oldest daughter Jessica made "Radiation Inspiration," 33 note cards inscribed with a special memory for each day of radiation. Like Judy, I could "write a book" about the love and support of my family and friends, the doctors God provided, the prayers offered on our behalf, the countless acts of kindness shown to us and how they humbled me and caused a flood of tears. The blessings are endless, but perhaps the greatest is coming to understand how people can say that an illness or tragedy is a blessing. I praise God and give Him the glory for allowing me to find the joy of cancer, to share this joy with others and have the joy of a new and deepening friendship with my sister in Christ, Judy. My prayer is you will allow Christ to walk each step of this journey with you so cancer can bless you knowing that "the joy of the Lord is **your** strength."

Pam Wilson
Inspiring Friend who is now cancer free

DR. JUDY J. STAMEY, retired church administrator and Christian educator serving churches for over 30 years in North Carolina and Texas. Presently, Judy serves as a church consultant, speaking frequently at workshops and conferences addressing Personnel and Staff Development issues in the church. She contributed several chapters in all three editions of the *Church Administration Handbook.*

Judy served five years as an adjunct professor in Church Administration at Southwestern Seminary in Fort Worth, Texas. In addition, she contributed to the development of the CBA Certification Program at Southwestern and served for twenty seven years as co-director and five years as director.

She received her B.A. in religious education from Gardner Webb University and her M.A. and Ph.D. in Church Administration from Southwestern Baptist Theological Seminary. Judy is certified in church administration by two national organizations: NACBA and SBCBAA.

Judy's honors include: Inducted by NACBA into the Hall of Fame, Distinguished Alumni by Gardner Webb University and Who's Who at both Gardner Webb and Southwestern Seminary.

Judy is married to Wade Stamey. They have 3 daughters: Lisa (deceased), Kim and Angel, 2 grandsons, and 1 granddaughter. Judy and Wade are members of Travis Avenue Baptist Church in Fort Worth, Texas